The S...

WESTWARD EXPANSION

WITHDRAWN

D1115864

By Greg Roza

Gareth Stevens
Publishing

Please visit our Web site, www.garethstevens.com. For a free color catalog of all our
high-quality books, call toll free 1-800-542-2595 or fax 1-877-542-2596.

Library of Congress Cataloging-in-Publication Data

Library of Congress Cataloging-in-Publication Data

Roza, Greg.
  Westward expansion / Greg Roza.
    p. cm. — (The story of America)
  Includes index.
  ISBN 978-1-4339-4781-0 (pbk.)
  ISBN 978-1-4339-4782-7 (6-pack)
  ISBN 978-1-4339-4780-3 (library binding)
  1. United States—Territorial expansion—Juvenile literature. 2. West (U.S.)—History—Juvenile
literature. 3. West (U.S.)—Discovery and exploration—Juvenile literature. 4. Frontier and
pioneer life—West (U.S.)—Juvenile literature. I. Title.
  F591.R79 2011
  978'.02–dc22

                                        2010040070

First Edition

Published in 2011 by
Gareth Stevens Publishing
111 East 14th Street, Suite 349
New York, NY 10003

Designer: Daniel Hosek
Editor: Therese Shea

Photo credits: Cover, pp. 1, 4, 5, 6, 7, 12–13, 14–15, 16–17, 18, 19, 20, 23 (Pony Express), 24,
26–27 MPI/Getty Images; pp. 8, 10, 29 Fotosearch/Getty Images; pp. 9, 13 (Austin), 21, 25
Hulton Archive/Getty Images; p. 17 (Polk) Stock Montage/Getty Images; pp. 22–23 Timothy
H. O'Sullivan/Getty Images.

Printed in the United States of America

CPSIA compliance information: Batch #CW11GS: For further information contact Gareth Stevens, New York, New York at 1-800-542-2595.

Contents

Words in the glossary appear in **bold** type the first time they are used in the text.

A Growing Nation

On September 3, 1783, representatives from Great Britain and the newly formed United States of America signed the Treaty of Paris. This document formally ended the American Revolution. It also made the Mississippi River the western boundary of the United States. With the war behind them and a need for money, the U.S. government turned its eyes toward the frontier west of the original 13 colonies.

Native Americans—shown watching settlers arrive by boat—were forced to move again and again as Americans spread across the country.

The Treaty of Paris represented the beginning of an exciting time in U.S. history—the age of westward expansion. During this time, the U.S. government obtained more and more land in western North America. Citizens and **immigrants** traveled west and settled land continually until the United States stretched "from sea to shining sea."

Land Ordinances

Once the United States became a free country, the U.S. government needed to raise funds. The organization and sale of frontier land became a key way to do this. Several land **ordinances** in the late 1700s established laws for measuring, distributing, and settling this land. They also divided the frontier into square "townships." One township in every territory was set aside as a school district. Land ordinances helped speed up frontier settlement.

the United States after the Treaty of Paris ▶

5

The Louisiana Purchase

By 1800, many U.S. settlers—mostly merchants, trappers, loggers, and farmers—relied heavily on the Mississippi River and the port of New Orleans for transportation and **commerce**. Many Americans had even settled in areas west of the Mississippi, which Spain had recently sold to France. President Thomas Jefferson quickly recognized how important the river, port, and western lands were to the future of the U.S. economy.

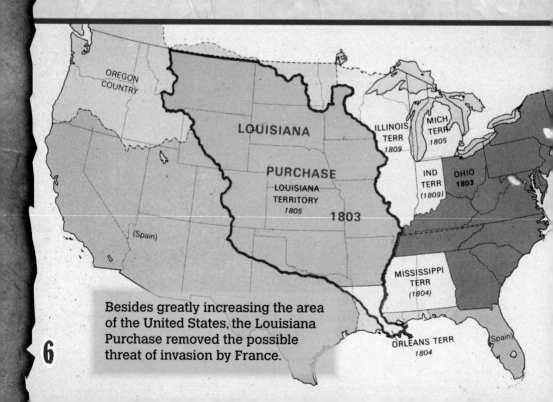

Besides greatly increasing the area of the United States, the Louisiana Purchase removed the possible threat of invasion by France.

In 1801, Jefferson sent a representative to France to purchase the port and receive permission to use the river. At first, France refused. However, 2 years later, French officials surprised Jefferson by offering to sell the entire Louisiana Territory to the United States for $15 million. With the Louisiana Purchase, Jefferson doubled the size of the United States.

The Corps of Discovery

In 1803, President Jefferson organized the **Corps** of Discovery to explore the Louisiana Territory. Army officers Meriwether Lewis and William Clark led the small expedition over thousands of miles of uncharted land. The corps mapped a route to the Pacific Ocean and befriended Native Americans along the way. They recorded information about the land and wildlife they encountered as well. The expedition helped to raise interest in settling land in the untamed west.

DID YOU KNOW?

The United States bought the Louisiana Territory for less than 5 cents an acre.

7

The Erie Canal

While many citizens became interested in settling in the western frontier in the early 1800s, travel was difficult and often dangerous. Transporting supplies to the West—and transporting resources back East—was costly and time consuming. Railroads were growing rapidly, but the government was looking for other ways to make transportation easier and less expensive. To some, canals seemed to be the answer.

The building of the Erie Canal was a major feat. This crew works in Lockport, New York.

This picture shows the famous "flight of five" locks in Lockport, New York, after the canal's completion.

The Impact of the Erie Canal

The completion of the Erie Canal marked the first great western **migration** of American settlers. It was the United States' first east–west water route. The canal's impact on western settlement, transportation, and commerce was immediate. Buffalo quickly became a vital destination for midwestern farmers who needed to ship wheat to the East and receive supplies from New York City. In short, the Erie Canal helped both western farms and eastern cities to thrive.

Completed in 1825, the Erie Canal in New York State linked the Hudson River to Lake Erie. The canal instantly made it easier, quicker, and cheaper to travel to and from the frontier west of the Appalachian Mountains. It also convinced more easterners to settle out West. Locations along the canal—such as Albany, Syracuse, Rochester, and Buffalo—quickly grew into important cities.

DID YOU KNOW?

The Erie Canal was 363 miles (584 km) long. It used 83 **locks** to raise and lower ships between stretches of water of different levels.

Manifest Destiny

By the 1830s, it had become clear to many Americans that westward expansion was beneficial for the United States. The West had seemingly limitless natural resources, and more resources meant more money for the growing nation. As more people moved west, the idea of Manifest Destiny became more popular.

This painting shows a beautiful spirit, a symbol of Manifest Destiny, leading settlers into the West.

Manifest Destiny was the belief that the United States had a mission to extend its western border all the way to the Pacific Ocean. Many people credit journalist John L. O'Sullivan for coining the term in 1845. However, the idea had steadily grown more popular throughout the previous decade. Manifest Destiny became a popular national **motto**. It was used by those who supported political and military missions to expand the borders of the United States.

John L. O'Sullivan

John L. O'Sullivan was the founder of *United States Magazine and Democratic Review*. In an 1845 editorial, he supported the **annexation** of Texas. He also wanted the United States to claim California and extend the western border to the Pacific Ocean. O'Sullivan wrote that other countries sought to limit the greatness of the United States by "checking the fulfillment of our manifest destiny to overspread the continent allotted by **Providence** for the free development of our yearly multiplying millions."

DID YOU KNOW?

"Manifest" is another word for "obvious." The term "destiny" refers to an event or a series of events that will—without doubt—happen in the future.

Texas Joins the United States

Texas was once part of New Spain and later part of Mexico. In 1820—one year before Mexico gained its freedom—Spain began allowing **Anglo-Americans** to settle in Texas. Over the next 15 years, thousands of Anglo-Americans settled there. Many of the settlers believed that the United States would soon buy eastern Texas from Mexico, and they hoped to be U.S. citizens once again in the near future.

After winning a war with Mexico in 1836, Texas declared itself an independent nation. However, Texas struggled to defend itself against Mexico. Its economy also struggled. Some members of the Texas government asked the U.S. government to annex Texas. In 1845, the U.S. Congress agreed to make Texas the twenty-eighth state in the Union. This move angered the Mexican government, which had never recognized Texas's independence.

The Battle of the Alamo in 1836 was one of the most famous battles in Texas's struggle for independence.

Moving to Texas

In 1820, Moses Austin became the first Anglo-American to receive approval from Spanish officials to settle land in Texas. He died soon after. His son, Stephen Austin, took over the land grant. Austin was originally granted enough land for 300 families. Anglo-American settlement of the area gained energy in the next decade. By 1836, the population of Texas had reached 50,000 people. In 1847, Texas was home to 142,000 American citizens.

◀ Stephen Austin

DID YOU KNOW?

The Republic of Texas was weakened by two arguing political groups. One wanted to join the United States. The other wanted to remain free and extend the western border of Texas to the Pacific Ocean.

The U.S.-Mexican War

Rumors of a war with Mexico began stirring soon after Texas became a state. Many U.S. citizens complained that the country had no right to kill Mexicans and take their land. Others, however, believed Mexico was at fault for owing the United States money and never acknowledging Texas's independence. President James K. Polk—who had become president in 1844—viewed the war as a

Future U.S. president Zachary Taylor leads American soldiers into battle at Palo Alto during the U.S.-Mexican War.

chance to gain important land in the West.

In April 1846, Mexican troops crossed the Rio Grande to attack American forces in southern Texas, officially starting the U.S.-Mexican War. Battles during the war took place in Texas, California, and Mexico. In September 1847, U.S. forces reached Mexico City. Soon after, Mexico surrendered.

The Treaty of Guadalupe Hidalgo

On February 2, 1848, U.S. and Mexican officials signed the Treaty of Guadalupe Hidalgo, which officially ended the U.S.-Mexican War. The treaty added 1.2 million square miles (3.1 million sq km) to the United States—an area that includes most of the southwestern United States. In return, the United States gave Mexico $15 million.

DID YOU KNOW?

In 1853, the United States paid Mexico for another 30,000 square miles (77,700 sq km) of land in southern Arizona and New Mexico. This was called the Gadsden Purchase.

The Oregon Territory

The Oregon Territory was an area of land in the Pacific Northwest that included the modern states of Oregon, Washington, and Idaho, as well as parts of Montana and Wyoming. Both the United States and Great Britain claimed this area.

Once again, President Polk was at the forefront of the push to make this area part of the United States.

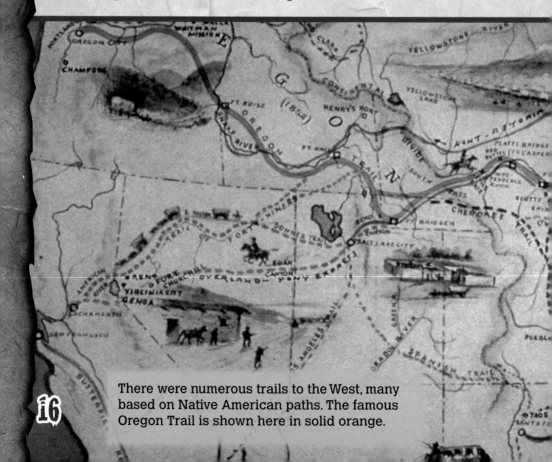

There were numerous trails to the West, many based on Native American paths. The famous Oregon Trail is shown here in solid orange.

Instead of using the military, as he did when dealing with Mexico, Polk chose to use **diplomacy** with Great Britain. In 1846, the British signed the Oregon Treaty. This document made the 49th **parallel** the northern border of the United States. Over the next few years, many pioneers from the East came to settle in Oregon. The population grew rapidly.

The Oregon Trail

By 1846, many pioneers had already settled in the Oregon Territory. Most reached the area by means of an overland route that came to be called the Oregon Trail. It started in Missouri and ended more than 2,000 miles (3,200 km) away in Oregon's Willamette Valley. Travel on the Oregon Trail was dangerous. Some pioneers died along the way. Those who made it, however, found rich land for farming.

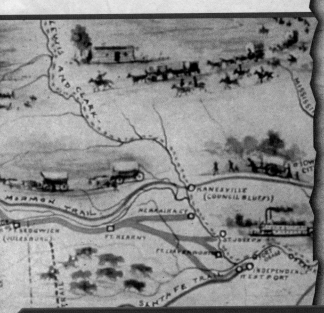

James Polk ▷

17

The Mormon Migration

Mormons are members of a religious group that got its start in 1830 in Fayette, New York. Although membership in the church grew quickly, many people didn't like the new religion. Mormons were forced to head west in search of a friendlier place to live. From

This illustration shows the Mormons arriving in Salt Lake Valley, located in what is now Utah.

1839 to 1846, most Mormons lived in Nauvoo, Illinois. However, hostilities against Mormons soon forced them to head further west.

Mormon leaders, including Brigham Young, selected the Salt Lake region of today's Utah as their final destination. The Mormon migration took place between 1846 and 1847. After a difficult journey, 148 Mormons—including Brigham Young—founded Salt Lake City on July 24, 1847. They became the first non–Native Americans to settle in this area.

The Mormon Trail

To get from Illinois to Salt Lake Valley, the Mormons traveled a path that became known as the Mormon Trail. The first stretch of the trail led from Nauvoo to Fort Kearney in the Nebraska Territory, where the trail linked up with a long stretch of the Oregon Trail. At Fort Bridger in today's Wyoming, the Mormon Trail separated from the Oregon Trail and headed southwest to Salt Lake City. Altogether, the Mormon Trail was about 1,300 miles (2,090 km) long.

◄ Brigham Young

DID YOU KNOW?

Between 1847 and 1869, nearly 70,000 Mormons traveled to Utah along the Mormon Trail.

The Rush for Riches

The dream of Manifest Destiny had been achieved by the late 1840s. The United States stretched from the Atlantic to the Pacific. However, much of the West was still uninhabited frontier land. Although many people knew the West was full of natural resources, it was the quest for immediate riches that hastened population growth.

In 1848, gold was discovered in California. News spread across the nation and around the globe quickly. In 1849, people began flocking to the site in hopes of becoming rich. Most people didn't find their fortune in the goldfields. However, many of them decided to settle in California, and the population rose quickly. In very few years, several California settlements grew into important cities.

Sacramento, shown here in 1850, was established as a mining town just 2 years earlier. Today, it's California's capital city.

DID YOU KNOW?

The year 1852 marked the height of gold rush immigration. About 67,000 people came to California that year, and 20,000 were from China.

Immigrants in California

U.S. citizens weren't the only people to travel to California during the gold rush. Immigrants came from many places, including Mexico and South America. One of the largest groups of immigrants came from China. In fact, many Chinese fortune hunters arrived in California before the word had even reached the eastern United States. Although most immigrants were treated poorly, they left a lasting impression on the settlement of the western frontier.

As the California gold rush died down, miners searched other western areas for gold. In 1859, a rich deposit of silver ore was found on Mount Davidson in the Utah Territory (in the region that's now Nevada). Henry Comstock claimed to own the land, so the deposit became known as the Comstock **Lode**. News about the find spread quickly. Soon miners from around the world rushed to the area.

Nearby "boomtowns," such as Virginia City, grew quickly as people came to strike it rich. For

This photo shows Virginia City, Nevada, in 1867. The Gould and Curry Mine Mill constructed many of these buildings for their operations.

close to 20 years, miners continued to find silver. In time, however, just as with the gold in California, the Comstock Lode ran out. Many of the boomtowns of the past dwindled as miners left for other areas. However, many other people settled down nearby.

The Pony Express

Just after the Comstock Lode was discovered, three enterprising men started a mail service connecting the East and the West. The Pony Express used a system of fast horses and able riders to carry messages from St. Joseph, Missouri, to Sacramento, California, in about 10 days. Although it was soon replaced by the telegraph, for 19 months the Pony Express was the "high-speed connection" between the East and the West.

DID YOU KNOW?

Virginia City began as a "**shanty** town" where miners set up poorly constructed homes. It soon became the second-largest city in the West with more than 20,000 residents!

Free Land!

In 1862, just after the beginning of the American Civil War, President Abraham Lincoln signed the Homestead Act into law. This act was designed to encourage citizens to settle on the Great Plains and improve the land there by farming on it. Each settler was given 160 acres of federally owned land for their family. The settler had to live on and farm the land for 5 years before they became the legal owners. Or, after living on the land for 6 months, they could buy it for $1.25 an acre.

This family, shown in Nebraska, is traveling to a homestead obtained through the 1862 land act.

The Homestead Act of 1862 was a great success. Many citizens took advantage of the deal. By 1900, the government had distributed 80 million acres of federally owned land to settlers. The act remained in effect until 1976.

DID YOU KNOW?

Ten percent of the land in the United States—a total of 270 million acres—was settled because of the Homestead Act of 1862.

The Difficult Life on a Homestead

Homestead life on the Great Plains was hard. Many of the people who took advantage of the offer of free land were not farmers. Much of the land was dry, dusty, and not well suited to farming. Irrigating the land was expensive. In some areas, dust storms made homestead life unbearable. Less than half of the people who filed claims for land actually received land deeds after 5 years. Some settlers traveled from one area to another until they found a better situation.

house on a homestead

The Rise of Cattle

In the 1500s, the Spanish brought European cattle to Mexico. The herds grew enormous. Many types of cattle ran wild. In time, the herds had spread up into Texas. By the 1860s, there were about 5 million **longhorns** in Texas.

After the Civil War, the demand for meat in the East and West grew. Cattle worth $10 a head in

This image is a dramatic illustration of a cattle drive through Dodge City, Kansas.

Texas could sell for 20 times more on the West Coast. Texas ranch owners raised tens of thousands of longhorns on vast ranches. Several times a year, they hired cowboys to lead cattle drives. Cowboys led the cattle north along cattle trails to railroad stations hundreds of miles away. Many of the "cow towns" where north–south cattle trails and east–west railroads met grew into important cities.

Abilene, Kansas

One of the most important cow towns was also the first—Abilene, Kansas. A railroad was built through the tiny town in 1867. Illinois businessman Joseph G. McCoy recognized the railroad could transport Texas cattle east. He set up a **stockyard** and a hotel. Texas ranchers soon began leading their herds to Abilene on the Chisholm Trail. Filled with cowboys and railway men, Abilene was a dangerous place. However, the tiny town flourished quickly.

DID YOU KNOW?

Between 1866 and 1890, more than 5 million head of cattle were driven north on cattle trails. By that time, more railroads and refrigerated railcars made cattle drives unnecessary.

The Transcontinental Railroad

Throughout the first half of the 1800s, the construction of railroads in the Northeast was steady and productive. At first, railroads were built between relatively close cities. Soon, these smaller railroads were connected to form an ever-growing rail network crisscrossing the eastern half of the country. The West, however, was untouched by railroads.

On May 10, 1869, the first **transcontinental** railroad in the United States was completed. The line connected the East and West, making travel easier, safer, and quicker. It sped up the rate at which the West was populated, bringing more and more settlers

Timeline

1783
Great Britain and the United States sign the Treaty of Paris

1803
The United States buys the Louisiana Territory from France

1820
Moses Austin is given permission to settle in Texas

1836
Texas wins a war with Mexico and becomes a free nation

1845
Texas becomes the twenty-eighth state in the United States

1784
Congress passes the first land ordinance

1803
President Thomas Jefferson organizes the Corps of Discovery to explore the Louisiana Territory

1825
The Erie Canal is completed

1845
John L. O'Sullivan uses the term "manifest destiny" in print for the first time

every year. Soon travelers could reach just about any location in the United States on newly built railroads. The era of westward expansion was drawing to an end.

The transcontinental railroad was built across difficult terrain, making it easier than ever to reach the West.

1846
Great Britain and the United States sign the Oregon Treaty

1847
The U.S.-Mexican War ends; the first Mormons arrive in the Utah Territory

1848
U.S. and Mexican representatives sign the Treaty of Guadalupe Hidalgo

1849
The California gold rush begins

1853
The United States acquires more territory through the Gadsden Purchase

1859
Miners find the Comstock Lode in the Utah Territory

1862
Congress passes the Homestead Act

1866
The era of cattle trails begins

1869
The first U.S. transcontinental railroad is completed

Glossary

Anglo-American: an American of European descent who settled in Mexican Texas

annexation: the addition of land to a country or region

commerce: the large-scale buying and selling of goods and services

corps: a group of people who work together to accomplish a task

diplomacy: peaceful communication between nations

immigrant: someone who moves into a new country from another country

lock: a device for raising and lowering ships between stretches of water that are different levels

lode: a deposit of ore

longhorn: a breed of cow with long horns once common in Texas

migration: the act of moving from one area to another

motto: a short saying that expresses a rule to live by

ordinance: a law or rule

parallel: an imaginary line around Earth that is always the same distance away from the equator

Providence: guidance from God

shanty: a poorly built shack

stockyard: an enclosed yard where livestock are kept

transcontinental: extending across a continent

For More Information

BOOKS

Landau, Elaine. *The Oregon Trail*. New York, NY: Children's Press, 2006.

Mountjoy, Shane. *Manifest Destiny: Westward Expansion*. New York, NY: Chelsea House Publishers, 2009.

Steele, Christy. *Famous Wagon Trails*. Milwaukee, WI: World Almanac Library, 2005.

WEB SITES

The Erie Canal Museum
www.eriecanalmuseum.org
The Erie Canal Museum Web site has information, videos, games, and more to help you learn about the historic canal.

Gold Rush!
pbskids.org/wayback/goldrush
Discover what life was like for gold miners in California.

Lewis & Clark: The Journey of the Corps of Discovery
www.pbs.org/lewisandclark
Explore numerous resources about the Corps of Discovery.

Index